Yummmmm!

What's in the fridge?

S0-AXP-133

FOOD FREEZER

Chiller

Science Fair™ Cottage Cheese

SMUCKER'S Strawberry Preserves

Stick the food stickers from
page 3 onto this page.

1

C over all the
X's with
food stickers
from page 3.

2

Stick these stickers on pages 1 and 2.

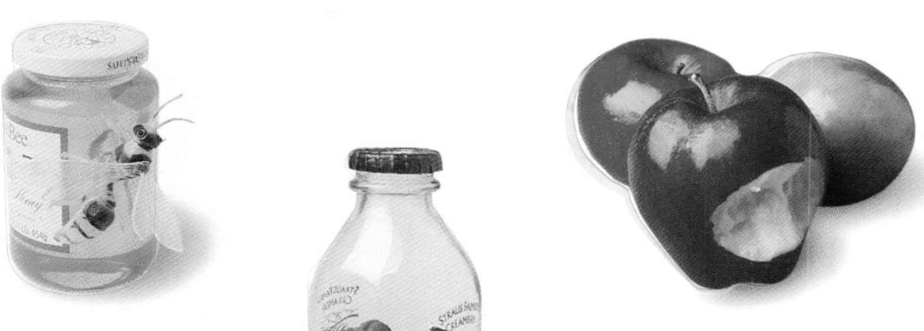

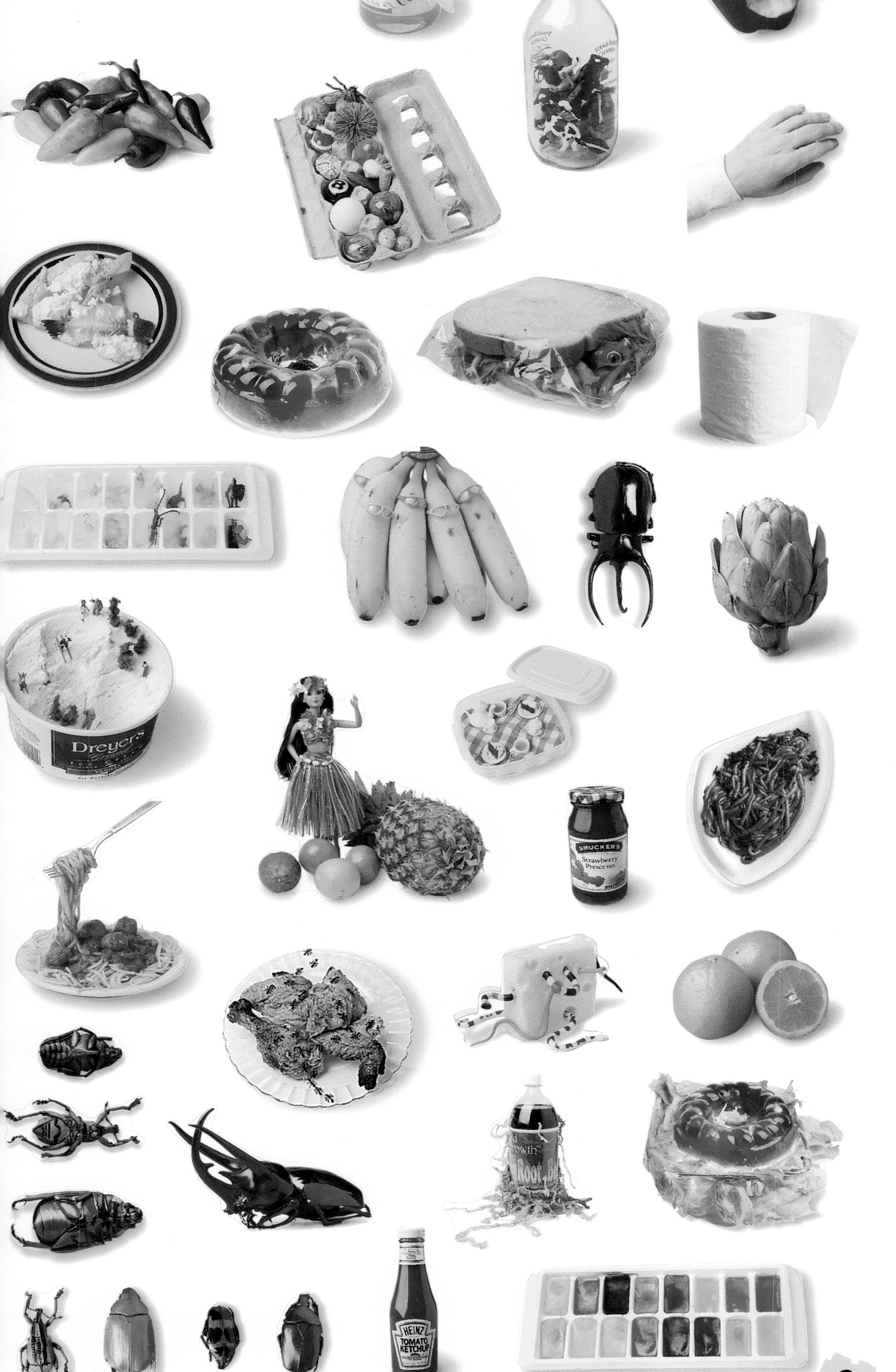

Stick these stickers on page 6.

These are the robot parts that go onto the robot on page 5.

4

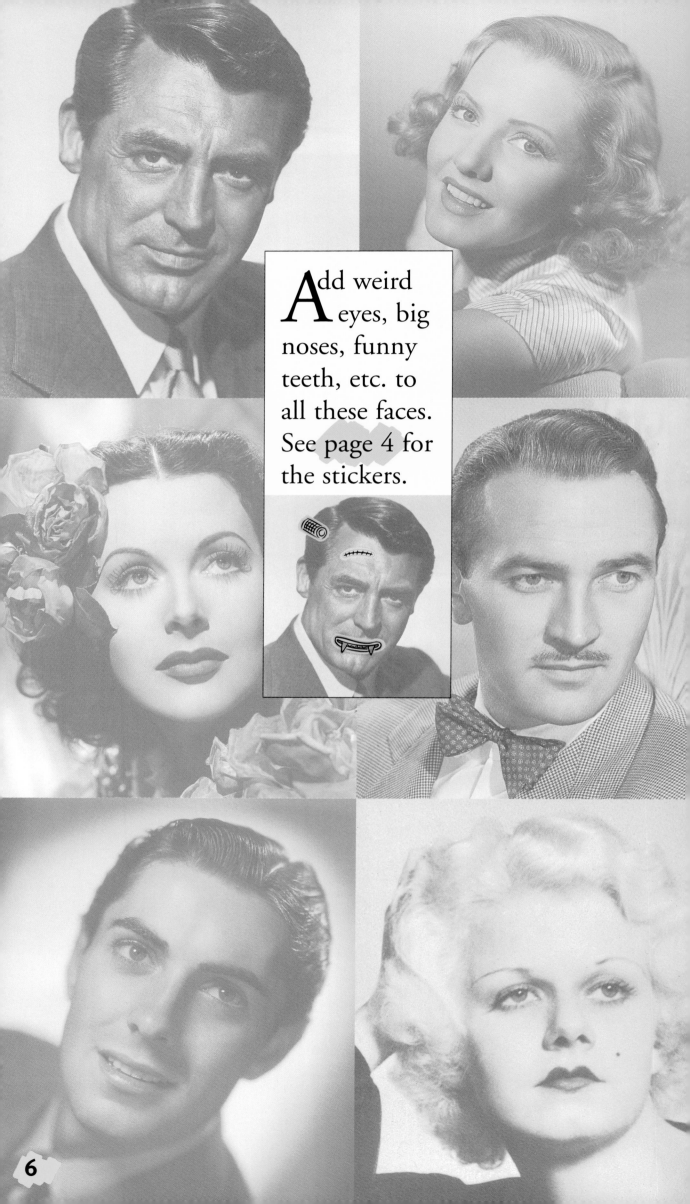

Add weird
eyes, big
noses, funny
teeth, etc. to
all these faces.
See page 4 for
the stickers.

W hat to wear? Use the stickers from page 9 and put some clothes on these kids.

Use the stickers from the top of page 9 to cover up these ✖'s in these cartoons.

Stick these stickers on page 8.

These are clothes for the kids on page 7.

These are all the baby animal stickers that go on page 13.

These are all the star stickers that go on page 12.

These are all the beauty shop stickers that go on page 11.

GeL

10

Use the beauty shop stickers from page 10. Stick them wherever you think they should go.

U se the star stickers
from page 10.
Sprinkle them all
over this page.

U se the baby animal stickers on page 10. Put the right baby with the right parent (stick them down on the X's).

x

x

X

X

x

X

x

X

Add feathers, antlers, eyes, wings, etc. All the parts you'll need are on page 15.

15

These stickers go with the cartoons on page 17.

These face stickers go onto the pictures and paintings on pages 18 and 19.

EEK!

I'M YOUR substitute TEACHER.

JIMMY is playing with ME.

Use the stickers from page 16 to cover up the ✖'s.

I'd like you to MEET MY fiancé.

This is YOUR babysitter tonight.

CONGRATULATIONS it's a   .

17

Get the weird face stickers from page 16. Use them to cover up all the regular faces in these pictures.

Fill this gumball machine with all the toy stickers from page 21.

These vegetables go in the garden on page 23.

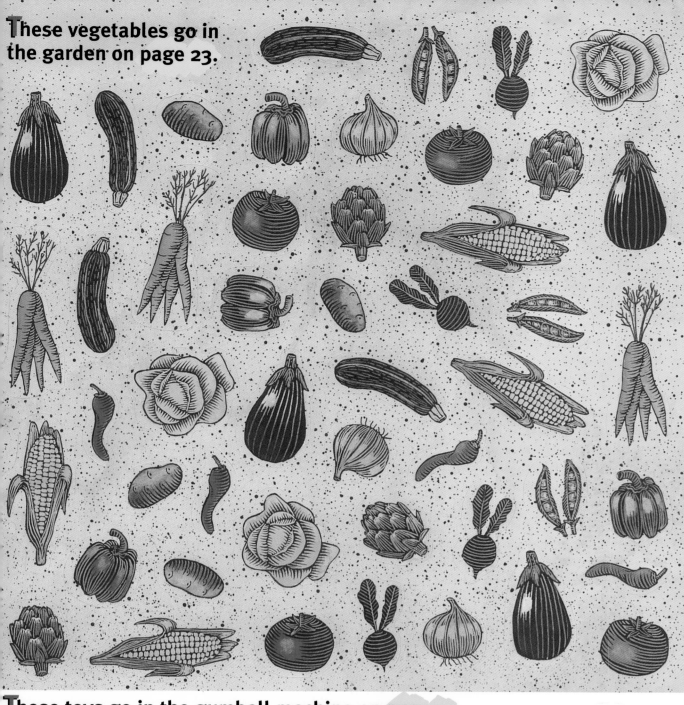

These toys go in the gumball machine on page 20.

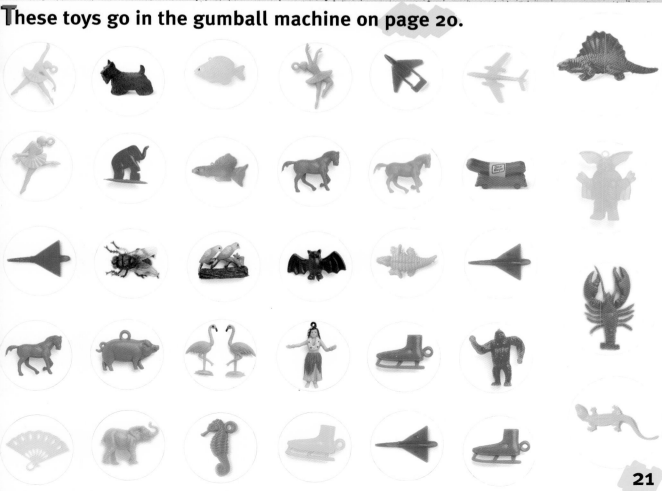

21

Put these fish in the aquarium on page 25

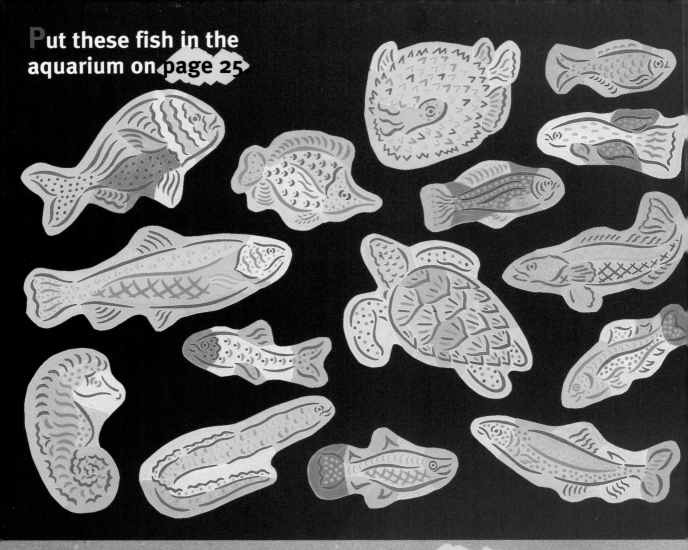

Put these car stickers in the car lot on page 24.

P ut the vegetable stickers from page 21 in this garden.

Put the STRANGE car
stickers from Page 22
in this lot.

P ut the fish stick-
ers from page 22
into this
aquarium.

These are the instructions for folding and making triangle envelopes (they work as well as regular ones!). To decorate them, use the stickers from page 27.

2. Next, with a straight edge, draw a triangle inside the circle. Try to make every side the same length.

3. Fold along the three lines. Put a little circular note inside and tuck the three flaps together. Seal shut (and decorate) with stickers.

4. Write the address on the backside, put a postage stamp on it, and drop in the mail.

Syringa Rose Volk
2121 Staunton Court
Palo Alto, CA 94306

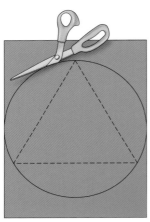

1. Start with a piece of colored construction paper. Put an upside-down bowl on the paper and use it to draw a circle. Then, cut the circle out.

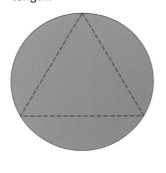

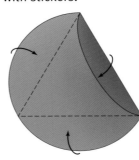

Use all of these stickers to decorate your envelopes
(page 26), pop-ups (page 28), and boxes (page 30).

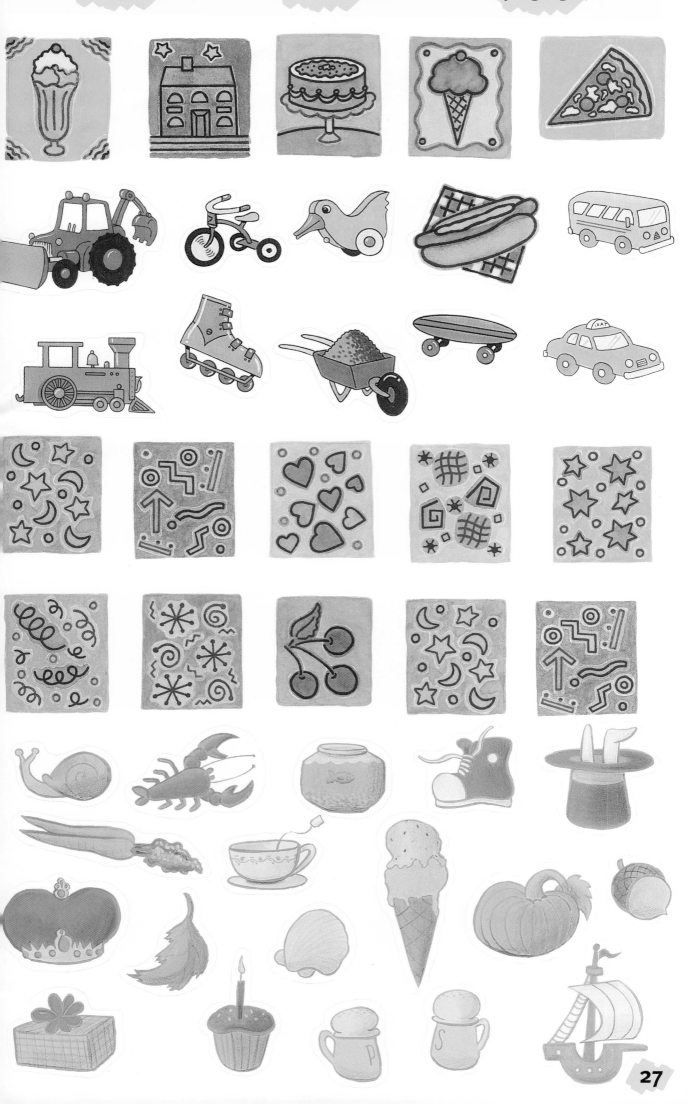

Tricky Stickies

Carefully put each of these stickers on real dollar bills, real envelopes, real soup cans, real cereal boxes and real bananas.

Put these stickers onto cereal boxes and bananas.

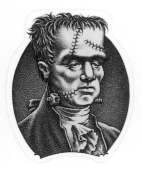

Put these over George on any $1 bill.

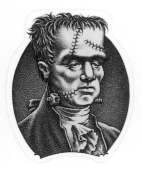

Add these to any letters you're mailing.

Put these stickers onto soup cans.